MOVING TOWARDS LIGHT

Moving Towards Light

Cynthia Fuller

Acknowledgements

Some of these poems have appeared in the following magazines and books: *Iron; Keywords; The Literary Review; Poetry Durham; Women's Review; Writing Women; New Women Poets*, ed. Carol Rumens (Bloodaxe Books, 1990); *Poems 88* (Lancaster Literature Festival, 1988); *Poets' Voices* (Tübingen/Durham Poets' Exchange, Kulturamt Tübingen, 1991); *Wordlife*, ed. Angel and Patrick Scott (Nelson, 1988). The author is grateful to all the editors involved.

The coloured etching reproduced on the front and back covers is *Cow Parsley* by Della Chapman.

The photograph of Cynthia Fuller is by Chris McNulty.

Flambard Press wishes to thank Northern Arts for its financial support.

Published in 1992 by Flambard Press
4 Mitchell Avenue, Jesmond, Newcastle upon Tyne NE2 3LA

All rights reserved. No part of this publication may be reproduced, stored in a retrieval system or transmitted in any form, or by any means, electronic, mechanical, photocopying, recording or otherwise, without the prior permission of the publisher.

A CIP catalogue record for this book is available from the British Library.

ISBN 1 873226 02 0

© Cynthia Fuller

Cynthia Fuller has asserted her right to be identified as the author of this work.

Typeset by Writers Inc, Newcastle upon Tyne
Cover design by Peter Morrill
Printed in Great Britain by Athenaeum Press, Newcastle upon Tyne

Contents

1	Beginning
2	Woodwork
3	My Grandmother
4	Warehouse
5	Scars
6	Images
8	To My Sister
10	Going Back
12	Fictions
14	Changes
15	Islands
16	After the Joan Eardley Exhibition
17	Barbara Hepworth's Studio, St Ives
18	Gwen John: A Lady Reading
20	Haworth Parsonage, 31 March
21	Flower Painting: Georgia O'Keeffe and Winifred Nicholson
22	Ondine
24	Sleeping Beauty
25	Cassandra
26	Witness
28	Her Story
29	History
30	Survival
31	Now
32	Visiting Germany
33	In Peacetime
34	Encounter
36	To My Sons
37	Rainbows
38	Words and Stone
39	Mid-way
40	Pool
41	Self-centre
42	Purpose

43	Birds
44	After the rain
46	Impossibilities
47	Desire
48	Travelling
49	Parting
50	Norfolk Fragments
52	Berwick Clifftop, May
53	Blue Birds
54	Altitude
55	Dream
56	No Flowers
57	Ridge
60	An Autumn Journal
62	Conversation
63	Crossing the Edge
64	Letting Love Back
65	Prayer at the Year's Ending

Beginning

Being roused, uncurled,
squeezed tight along the tunnel,
pushed out from warm blood walls
from darkness into glare,
cold open space;
bones giving, lungs thinning,
sounds beating, touch bruising,
throat and mouth opening
to the taste of our own cry —
we do not remember this.

Waking suddenly, being snapped
from sleep to consciousness
I have felt grief tight in my chest,
a cold grey weight I want to howl
out of its deep lodging, an old pain.
Beginning came before we had
the words to tame it with.
Hurtled again across that line
from not-knowing to knowing
I understand that it is safer to forget.

Woodwork

On winter nights my father worked in wood.
Coke sighed and crackled in the Rayburn,
dusty cats lay limp with heat,
Home Service voices spoke to us.
I watched the slow lead pencil trace
elaborate blueprints of his mind.
He measured, marked,
he stroked the surface of the wood,
touching the edges of his table
as if it was already there.

Sticking at first the saw would settle
to a regular raucous breathing, in and out.
The gritty rub of sandpaper,
the plane's sharp blade
sent falling drifts of pale sweet sawdust,
brittle ringlets of creamy wood.
Each cigarette's slow crumble into ash
became a scattering of soft grey flakes,
unnoticed.

Forgotten in his vision
I watched the quiet births of trolleys, tables, trays,
I watched his single-mindedness, his dreams.
He absorbed me in his concentration,
unknown to him it wrapped me round,
sheltered me from night time
and the cold dark house beyond that room.

My Grandmother

Only once he said I was like his mother.
It was my hair — he wanted me to keep it long
like hers; he said it was her colour.
I kept the words, hoarded them,
uneasy keepsakes of an absence.

No more to go on than the colour of her hair
I cannot see her, my father's mother.
Unsettled, I want to question her,
I want to know what single-minded love it was
that turned her face towards the wall
in mourning for her elder son,
what grief entombed her
with his soldier's death,
closing her eyes upon the child.

The link weighs heavy that he forged between us.
I do not remember if I wondered then
about the way I might betray him,
or only now I shrink from what it was
that she bequeathed me with her hair.

Warehouse

"Take the light. Be careful."
Afternoons in her father's store
transformed her, fascination stronger
than her fear of gaps and heights
and night, she climbed open stairs
into solid darkness
where the furniture reared in piles,
roped off in sections, named.

Drowning in silence, dust,
she shone the light
dredging a floral pattern,
carved legs, a bloated mattress;
drawn along passages,
braving bulging walls,
back to the furthest corner
where the roof leaked.

Damp furred the velvet,
white patches flowering
over polished surfaces,
split cushions spilling yellowing fluff,
blankets becoming holes, in chests.
She lifted the piano lid,
touched the notes to check
the music was still there.

"It's getting spoilt, that stuff."
As if he could halt it.
"It's been there years. They went
abroad. Never paid."
A life abandoned in a warehouse
mouldering and upside down.
She pictured them as unshelled snails
wandering abroad.

Scars

I found those china figures from your room,
pubescent girls, pink cheeks, lips pursed.
They wear their scars like amber necklaces.
A shoe became a missile hurtling rage,
daring the safety of our afternoons.
I do not remember that I broke them.

I remember your anger —
the casserole ricocheting off the wall
against his silence,
you scrubbing your hair with Daz
because he didn't like the colour,
the slammed doors and empty rooms,
the suitcase gone.

I remember the coolness of your room,
shiny curtains keeping out the sun,
the bedspread like pale tufts of grass.
Lying in soft green I would explore the boxes,
tip out bright treasures of brooches and buttons,
while you sat before the mirror
patting on a powder like sweet dust.

The girl who could let her body
arc and twist to kick her rage
I have forgotten.
The scar pulls tight on the edges of words,
it hurts to swallow all the time.
I have put your figures in my room.

Images

Scorning muted colours she sparkled
in scarlet, emerald green, kingfisher blue.
Anticipation of a dinner-dance
filled the house in steamy clouds
of Elizabeth Arden bath oil.
She moved in a rustle of shiny silk,
quick-footed in silver strapped sandals,
taut with excitement, already gone.

On windy Sundays
the house held its breath,
scarf billowing,
small frame bristling,
perched on the edges of open drains
she poked the springy lengths of wooden rods
deep in the earth,
perilously.
She tore at weeds, sliced hedges,
scattered like a whirlwind
the "blasted" cats who followed her.

Scorning the Archers she hid from us in books,
travelling out of the dingy room,
eyes skimming restless across the page.
Sometimes she played the piano
in wild erratic bursts,
her hard red nails clicking on the keys.
On bad days we would find her
standing tense in doorways,
hands clenched.

The house shrunk in when she was ill —
once she lay silent
the bedroom dark with anger and pain,
the dentist's botched job,
vivacity torn out with her teeth.
She climbed back into laughter,
holding an audience with anecdotes,
sitting on the edge of her chair,
wide-eyed and tightly sprung,
vibrant and glittering,
too restless to stay long.

To My Sister

We are each other's last connection
like last survivors
from another world.

Do you understand
when I say the house always smelt of dead birds —
close attics swum with the dizzy sweetness of it,
drifting impossibly through the bedrooms
from the quiet piles of feathers
in boarded-up chimneys.
If I think of starlings now they are always dead,
heaps of rainbow feathers dulling.
They chose to soot their colours in our chimneys
with all the sky to live in.
Were you afraid
when the wind made the poplar trees
tangle and crack,
shadows rattling on the bedroom wall,
while the roots grew silently.
Did you know that a pile of books made you tall enough
to see the sea through the attic window.
I could go to the sea anytime,
but it felt like magic to have it in the house,
when you needed it.

After we watched her die
I asked for the ring,
as if like the princess's in the story
it might carry an invisible thread
that spun back to her.
It works.
She holds the end tightly.

The ring is treasure
from a forgotten world.
Behind me there are ghosts and shadows
I must fill with colour;
dusty pictures
to be bright again.
The ring contains it all,
time past connecting us
and the lost world we have survived.

Going Back
Allonby, May 1982

   i   Against the odds
the house was there,
verandas shuttered to the wind
like eyes closed.
The cobbles and the beck were there,
white-painted bridges, just the same.
But wind and rain are hard on ghosts.
They try to melt them into salty air.

  ii   The distance from the butcher's shop had shrunk
from a morning's wandering to a stride —
Mother, I could bring the sausages so quickly now,
I wouldn't dawdle and you wouldn't weigh
my steps with your anxiety.

 iii   The girl who rode the pony
when its girth slipped round
until the world turned
upside down and beat
about her head with hooves
dared not cry.
She didn't dare refuse
the extra rides they gave
for being brave,
swallowed the knowledge
that she would slip again
and in the night
choked quietly on her fear.

iv   I found the past there
small and safe
against the odds.
Her Allonby stretched out its cobbled streets
and lay in sunshine through the August days.
I found a ghost town
salt with memories
holding them tight against the wind and rain.

Fictions

Suppose
she sits at a kitchen table
in the early morning looking out.
The door is open on the garden
clean and green from last night's rain.
The cat on the threshold washes
carefully over each black ear
as if she were not listening to the birds.
Neat window panes are dark with leaves —
honeysuckle tangles with ivy,
geraniums bloom untidy on the sill.
The room looks back at her,
papers half-full,
books half-read,
her papers, her life, unordered,
flowers in jam jars beginning to fade.

Or perhaps
it was the wind that woke her,
wrenching at the corners of the house.
The sea froths grey, gulls whip
diagonally, weightless,
spray spits ugly at the land.
She watches a boat —
brave blue and orange —
it drops down gullies,
is tossed on insubstantial crests.
As if the house had blown away
from round her, as if her life
lay squirming, silver bright and gasping,
she holds on to the jaunty bob of colour
willing its safe harbour.

But
she loses herself in busy streets.
Crowds knock their elbows through her skin,
her eyes turn inward filled with dirt.
Give her flowers and she'll revive.
Let her see hills folding one behind another,
a clear-day coastline when the waves
draw her through blue and blue
to rest in the violet of horizons.
Nothing is constant, she's a chameleon
who comes alive differently, depending
where you put her — at a kitchen table,
early; watching over a fishing boat.
Who is she in the darkness where no one sees,
her life held carefully like a sleeping child?

Changes

Her change to widow
changed me into friend.
I held her grief like heavy wool
for her to wind,
ached with importance,
a stiff friend
who dreamed her skirts grew wide enough
to hide in.
My love was nourished by safe walls.
Cut loose
I feared to fail her.

Islands

Dreaming of islands she saw the streets unwinding
into pale wide skies, buildings were cloud banks
smoke-thin and thick as down; the yellow neon
floated like a winter dawn in salt air,
each hill's brow promising the glint of water.

She dreamed a life with paths towards the sea,
an old stone house built low against the wind,
silencing the roars that might be engines,
guns, machines, hard shouts to break the night,
with the timeless suck and sigh of shingle.
She moved in quiet rooms, cocooned in colours
that she loved to touch, letting the silence
seep in, sifting, untangling the old tight knots.

Dreaming of islands that she could not reach
she traced the edges of her life.
From stony cul-de-sacs she saw a woman
climbing nimble-footed on wet rocks,
daring the sheer perimeters —
the very last rock and the current pulling.
Ahead she saw her, charting her boundaries,
a woman strong enough to cross cold seas.

After the Joan Eardley Exhibition

It was a bold vision
to take on sea and sky —
a life on the very edge,
in the teeth of the wind
where the waves break.

Close up her seas will drown you
in thick greys and whites,
then further back you see
the exact curling of the wave
foam poised specked with debris.

Cottages cling insubstantial
against the restless power
of air and water,
frail nets and boats
and a sky yellowing with storm.

In from the edge of things
she painted fields,
the elemental tempered,
foregrounds a delicacy
of flower heads and grasses.

Skies sing blue as kingfishers,
there is a sudden pink,
summer in lemon patches,
bold ripples of paint
become cornstalks and daisies.

It was a physical grappling
with what she saw —
the canvas large,
colours a rich crusting.
She set her easel on a cliff face
daring.

Barbara Hepworth's Studio, St Ives

Where light is liquid,
sea a slippery silver
as the sun comes up,
she took her mallets,
broke and chipped her art
from hard stone.
Where the skyline washes
out into the sea
her mind worked out
enduring curves
in solid wood.
Strong hands to cut through stone,
to turn and trace fine lines
from slabs of rock.
Her coats hang empty now,
the tools are still.
The dust has settled in her studio.
She has gone out,
her vision's sureness lasting ballast
against the brimming bay.

Gwen John: A Lady Reading

Before this moment there was movement.
Think, that she got up this morning.
She pulled the purple jumper, soft, over her head,
stepped into the heaviness of that full black skirt.
She brushed her hair, twisted it behind,
smoothed each light strand perfect.

Imagine, when she opened the window
she leaned out.
The peeling scars of buildings were the same,
the same sour air, brown water dripping,
dank corners slippery with soft shapes,
the silent crossing of a cat.

Bitter breeze from nowhere
billowed the curtain into the room,
a sudden cloud of red and white
pressing to her face like dusty skin.
She clutched its wild colours,
something rising in her throat.

Imagine her swirling,
the fabric sucking at the air,
her beating through the swell
for what would still the movement.
And then she found the bulky volume
and weighed the curtain down.

Think that her breathing was not easy.
She gripped the table's edge, the flimsy chair,
closed her eyes until the view inside
forced her to meet again
the empty room,
the shiver of the wallpaper's pale flowers.

She reached then for the small dark book,
let worn leather's comfort touch her fingers.
She found her place again.
Her closed face is a pale and perfect heart,
so still now.
The words begin to pull her in.

Haworth Parsonage, 31 March

Odd chance to choose that day to visit,
the knowledge of her dying that day
changing the ambience for always.
It had not seemed a dead house,
a museum cooping up dusty relics,
but full of words as if the walls absorbed
the talk that lasted late into the night;
a busy house — potato peeling, bread baking,
the German grammar propped against the bowl,
the desks, ink bottles, shelves of books.

Remnants of her vigour lie behind glass,
letters, the dried-up paints, beside
frail spectacles and haunting narrow shoes.
No gentle spring, the wind straight off the moors
still full of winter, a dark day.
Was she thinking of her legacy of heroines,
or of how much she had already lost?
Rooks circling the graveyard, building,
harsh harbingers with unrestful cries
for the ending of a life.

Flower Painting:
Georgia O'Keeffe and Winifred Nicholson

*Between them they gather
almost everything —*

In the heat petunia petals
fold back — such soft bloom —
the crease conjuring tongue,
shadowy centre deeper
than the black-purple
curling away.
She painted them
heavy with perfume
heady with desire
to touch
to brush the mouth
across such softness.

Breathing is easier here
in clear air —
a jar of wildflowers
and behind, the sea, the sky.
Picked flowers — their pink,
blue, white, as pure
as birdsong.
She painted infinity,
the horizon stretching
the flowers a moment
when petal becomes spirit,
colour light.

*— two women
looking at flowers.*

Ondine

It was the darkness drew me —
a sudden nightfall and the fish grew still,
water losing light, its colours draining;
shadow wedge across the sun,
blunt hook to lure the curious,
dark and heavy-baited.

In dreams I can remember
how the water held me.

Breaking the water's skin the first time
I felt the unknown rasp of air.
The man held out his hand,
standing between the sun and me.
Feet square set upon his earth
he drew me.

In dreams I can remember
how the water held me.

I did not know at first I could not breathe —
air is his element, I tried to be there,
slipping round the edges of his world.
Such kind hands, and something in me drying.
Our children have the sea drift in them,
their salt blue eyes awash with light.

In dreams I can remember
how the water held me.

The sea is dark today, ripples of indigo.
My clothes' rough weight lies on the stones.
The air is wet with salt and promises —
I have to go.
The smooth swell sighs against my skin,
sea silence closing over me.

In dreams I will remember
how he held me.

Sleeping Beauty

Hunching spider-like, rejected, she knew her business.
She planned it for the parents, her revenge,
the sharpened spindle a fit present for a princess.

The prick, the bloom of blood, and then escape.
Opening her eyes upon another world the princess saw
a landscape rich as tapestry, deep hills, a haze

heat-laden, soft on the horizon, ochre rocks, a dull green hollow
where solid beasts grazed, tree trunks twisting silver,
flakes of blossom drifting, square buildings safe in shadow.

She saw women working on the earth, bending to plant and gather,
women carrying from the shoreline rush baskets of bright fish,
women swinging axes, clearing ground, calling to each other.

Pollen-dusty butterflies, bright birds, a southern summer hush,
she lived and worked content among the almond trees, the olives.
Healed and strong she centred far from the good fairy's wish.

The sting came to her mouth and not her finger.
Blood burned in her cheeks, her shocked eyes opening
perceived a faded world, a pallid awkward youth,
a hundred-year-old hedge that needed cutting.

Cassandra

When he understood the power
he'd given her he spat
into her mouth, venom
seared, melted — not her vision,
her credibility.

She wandered the battlements,
her mind flickering
with wars and death.
The future smouldered in her words.
No one believed her.

This Cassandra's seventeen,
school-uniformed and urgent.
Her eyes are fire —
the Trojan battlements
a public speaking contest.

The words she speaks
conjure disaster,
a world that burns,
the gas shield torn,
her universe at risk.

She wins the prize —
for poise, delivery — not truth;
her words defused,
fierce prophecy diluted
in polite applause.

Witness

What the stories mean we cannot bear.
This is flimsy witness
images caught as the balance
swings between hope and despair.

*In the foreground camels,
in the background tanks;
the sky above the herdsmen
ripped apart by fire,
their beasts scatter,
the slow and certain rhythm
lost.*

There is no ending to the story.

*One said exploding tanks
were like fireworks,
colours fizzing
like fireworks;
excited, drunk with it,
high in the sky,
so high.*

What the stories mean we cannot bear.

*Boy on a bicycle,
the bicycle too large,
the boy with a mission
and a grin
like an unexpected crack of light,*

*wobbles his bone-shaker
away from the village
the elderly are putting
back together piece by piece,
into the desert
no longer deserted —
scrapyard, metal dump, grave.
He bristles with importance,
adventurer, scout,
pedalling into the desert,
sent looking for his brother,
soldier brother.*

There is no ending to the story.

Safe, we have witnessed
lives strained to the ragged edges.
There are many ways of lying.
We hide in words, tame horror
in the naming, play safe, fly high,
switch off before it hurts.
Scattered images are flimsy witness,
truth is hard to bear.

Her Story

Inside my head a woman
walking on a dusty road,
bare feet over baked earth,
flies hang in the heat.
Ahead the road bends.
I watch her.
There will be a gun-crack.
She will crumple,
a bundle of rags.
I will not be there.

I could write about the way
a fly tracks the black crack
of her mouth, about her hands
hardening in the sun.
I could write about what waits
at the beginning of her journey,
like a story.

I write the words.
I am not there.

I want to write
that she turns the corner,
finds water, shelter,
faces lifting, greeting,
home —
but that is not her story.

History

Then, it was the ticking by
of double lessons, dictated notes,
hollow chapters read aloud —
their only interest what we made
with our misreadings, secret jokes.
I never saw the minds behind
the acts, the faces hidden
by the neatly drawn crossed swords.
Odd words became pure sound
I'd idly taste — Herzegovina,
habeas corpus, Dreyfus, Bosnia —
all lives were kept so far
behind the barricades of dates
I never thought to look for them.

Years afterwards I stood within
a perfect circle as the sun went down.
Time telescoped. I touched a stone
that had been touched for more years
than my mind could hold. I saw
the past is as alive as we allow
it space to be, is never past.
The lumps of time they handed out
were fakes. Time is light and water,
a kaleidoscope of days and lives,
love and death, ambition, hate,
ideas, fear, power, integrity and dreams.
As we move forward the view behind us
shifts, we cannot hold it.

Survival

As if the land had shattered suddenly
islands are splinters adrift,
their rocks that were always there
bitten and edged by the salt winds.

Midsummer it is calm, the sea quiet.
The dunes are hollowed into gritty waves,
sand shifts and ripples, no firm foothold
for the drift of flowers, their unexpected perfume.

Land stretches back in even stripes
meticulously dug and turned to give its utmost;
today cows rustle warm in crumbling crofts
beside the crofters' modern bungalows.

High on the stony slopes green patches stand
memorial to settlers who hauled up
sand and seaweed to make that soil yield
grain, to coax a life from solid rock.

Rock, sand and salt endure
and in the churchyard on thin earth
fragments of teeth, of bones disturbed,
as if the bedrock is the surface here.

Now

Travelling forward we lug the past with us,
a collection of re-run slides, selected.
They come too easily to mind —
amateurs thumbprinting our negatives
we do not notice what the darkness hides.

There is a sort of bedrock in remembering
but the earth can slip, roots can be bared,
the ground around no longer stable.
The contours settle to another shape,
valleys where there were heights before.

Rootless, uncertain, we may stand
in a landscape that we cannot recognise,
not knowing where we'll go, or how we came,
there is only now to hold to,
who we are otherwise is left outside the frame.

Visiting Germany

I came encumbered by a luggage
I did not know how to leave behind.

I did not choose the stories —
my dead young soldier uncle
somewhere in the mud,
his mother gnawed away by loss.

The plane dipped towards beauty,
autumn landscape knows nothing of "enemy."

Then I remembered my father's story —
the pilot low flying by the road,
their eyes meeting, holding,
how he waited for the bomb that never came.

This Germany is yellow leaves against warm stone,
shared stories, words touching
tentative across the wonder
that our fathers did not kill each other.

In Peacetime

Over there, she told me, dawn sleep
explodes in splinters as they enter —
home turns nightmare —
the boots, the guns, the roaring,
slashed furniture, cupboards disembowelled,
storming the stairs to bayonet the mattresses,
then out into the night.
Home left gaping in the darkness.
Nothing to do but sweep together
what has been broken as best you can,
comfort your children back to sleep.

And here young men are practising.
Their blunt-nosed war machines bruise passage
through the valley's quiet —
slitting silence, breaking the dale apart
with terrible joy.
Nothing to do but wait until
the hills soak up the sound again
and nausea passes.
Nothing to do but trace the outline
of the hills' indifference
and wait.

Encounter

The steady drift of rain curtaining her
with the ducks, the dripping trees,
the river moving brown and full,
banks straggling with wet pinks,
the path slipping thick underfoot,
the rhythm of her walking mixing
in the pattering, small animal scuffling.

She saw rain peppering small circles
drawing fish to rise in larger rings,
a duck rolling wet beads over smooth back,
shovel-beak delicately preening
among overlapping browns and creams.

She felt the curl of wet ferns,
the clean mouths of balsam flowers,
beech trunks like stone,
water soaking into black earth
and the roots' deep tangle.

Ahead a blackbird's insistent cry —
she looked beyond the curtaining rain —
a figure running, arms spread for balance,
feet sliding, bruising into undergrowth,
running towards, and the bank shrinking,
flowers fading, and the river moving brown and full,
all rhythm lost in her heart's catch.

She saw the possibility of ending here —
rabbit-punched, knifed,
hands on her throat cutting off life —
button-eyed ducks would turn their heads
at her screams, would edge their brood
into the water, orange feet paddling.

She saw her body floating broken,
dragging at the reeds.
Flickering fish would mouth at her,
bob and nudge at swollen skin,
all that was left would sink then,
heavy and discoloured among the stones.

She watched him nearing,
breath tearing ragged, feet heavy,
dark hair slicked smooth, broad shoulders,
coat open, mouth loose for breathing,
young man running.
She did not see him — whose brother,
cousin, father, what woman's son —
only fear, bones near the surface,
blood beating, the possibility of ending here.

And he passing taking
the naked shock of it —
later he thought of the wild eyes
of a rabbit trapped in headlights.
Stumbling, off-balance,
not looking back, but remembering,
later it haunted him what she saw.

She listening to her heart
watched the moment pass with him.
No part of river now or morning,
all links lost she knew herself
caught in herself, alone.

To My Sons

You hold me on the cusp of hope and pain,
no curling safe into a female world —
a shell whose whorls and paths
slip smooth and cool as pearl —
I cannot leave you outside.

Other and familiar you are time
grown tangible, exuberant proof
that I was, as you push
your own way into yourselves,
leaving me behind.

I used to hold small hands,
bend to your level to point to —
I do not know how you see it now,
what you hear when the night
breaks with shouting, what you fear.

I want to say "Remember ..."
but the memories are safe.
Now has no protection,
your danger always my danger,
your gift to keep me here eyes open,
raw yet in hope, in trust.

Rainbows

Not looking out I almost missed the rainbow's
promise fading in a grey sky —
that promise that the waters would not rise again,
as if there would be an end to senseless death.

Today the newspapers print photographs
of children gassed, huddled bodies dropped
where they ran, wise in the dangers of war,
but innocent of that death's silent seeping.

Outside spring flowers are poised to bloom.
How many lives will end before
the buds can break with their new yellow,
what is it that the spring can signal now?

As if I could net hope I hung a crystal
in my window. Sunlight scuds bright rainbow
chips across the walls. No comfort.
Whatever used to hold it all together snapped.

The fragments scatter, I cannot hold them.
Birds sing and in dark cells the children scream.
How can I think of love when lives are beaten out,
who has the faith to scan the sky for rainbows?

Words and Stone

i If I took chisels, mallets,
scored and chipped away
until the stone held it —
rubbed and smoothed
a trunk of wood
to the shape that said it —
would you see what I meant,
could the grooves in the stone,
the grains in the wood catch it?

I want to hold a cry at the pitch
that will not let you shut it out,
etch on your retina the policeman's face
as he shoots into the running child.
Where are the mad with messages
urgent in the streets, the lost souls
who spoke through the crackle of their own flesh?

ii I want to write of hands that heal in darkness,
to write stories that end with forgiveness,
lost children found, bodies climbing out of ditches whole.

What can words do but warn, reflect or lie?
If a story whose ending broke against your mouth like joy
could make the world joyful I would tell it.

Till then I edge a way between fear and pain,
saying look what we are doing to the children,
holding like a pebble in my pocket
a fragment of dumb faith that we could be gentle too.

Mid-way

Horizons shifting outwards and outwards,
no closing yet, no angling of the light,
lines are clearer than I would have dreamed.

At twenty I saw this as a place of fear
where I might meet myself grown wise,
horizons shifting outwards and outwards.

I have not met her, that wise self.
What lodges here within this frame is all.
Lines are clearer than I would have dreamed.

So, what is different? What is learned?
Death leaves deep holes and friendship lasts,
horizons shifting outwards and outwards.

More time for detail, wonder that stirs
in the spread-fan colours of a bird's wing,
lines are clearer than I would have dreamed.

Love is not an answer — more a breathless path
between fear and joy, where I would learn to walk,
horizons shifting outwards and outwards,
lines are clearer than I would have dreamed.

Pool

I have been this way before,
the path jarring across hot rocks,
edges falling in a dusty scramble,
high cracks hung dry with rasps of plant;
the light too bright,
memory of yesterday's waves
engraved in hard sand lines.
I knew the midday tricks of sunlight,
sparkling a glint of water out of air.
I have been this way before.
Today the hard rocks opened on a pool
salt green and deep as any fantasy.
The water fits close.
The weed fronds cling
feathering against bare skin.
The light floats silver-wet
as the opal silk of oyster shells.
This is the touch my skin was aching for,
this is the place I never dared to dream.

Self-centre

Today I failed to see you
when the sun shone naked
from the bluest sky,
the water clear enough
to show the rocks.

The equivalent centre of self
George Eliot called it,
reserved her sharpest words
for those who missed it,
who only saw their own small selves.

In my scale too it weighs
like lead, this blindness,
a muddy kind of failure,
like crushing the fine blue
of a bird's egg underfoot.

Purpose

I watch the daylight rhythm of a blackbird,
life honed down to foraging and feeding,
beak fringed with grubs, her song muted.

There is seduction in simplicity,
as if the fragments could be pieced
into a pattern, could be whole.

Listen to the inner voice, they say, the soul.
But it is hard to hear above the other voices
clamouring, the shoulds, the dare-nots, wants.

Purposes are split, words indecisive.
I search for images of certainty, of faith,
the singleness of birds and saints.

Mr Takahashi is saving Japanese cranes,
incubating eggs, cherishing the flicker
that may drown in its own blood.

He feeds a chick — grubs clamped in tweezers,
he whistles to it, runs and flaps
until it lifts into the air away from him.

The cranes are dying out and he is saving them,
his soul soars high above him, singing.

Birds

I could believe that they are souls incarnate,
essential beings, refined and honed beyond
uncertainty, apology — there is nothing spare.

Singing they are vibrant in each nerve,
energy translating into music,
breath rolling into pure sound beads.

Existence is transcendent moments —
the blackbird becomes her wild alarm
pitting voice and wings against the hunter.

Gathering into flight the heron
barely lifts his length on heavy wings,
unwieldy progress, crane-fly legs trailing —

but landing he unfolds his neck
into sharp-eyed, sharp-beaked vigilance,
all still intensity at the water's edge.

If there is an essence at the centre,
some clarity deep buried in
the soft confusion of being human,

I would dream its metamorphosis
into bird, a sharp-edged life,
a being concentrated in song,
gathered to the soaring certainty of flight.

After the rain

white petals clench
harebells bend
heavy.

Springs froth
over silence
rock turns jet.

On the path
the rowan berries
splash blood.

I have been walking
tunnels of words
heavy-footed,

forgetting the lift
as mist parts,
the zing of vertigo.

Forgive me.

It is not
an infidelity —
not one to last.

I will come back.
Rocks have held
more than pain.

Not hill-wise enough
to be alone here
yet

I will come back
to trace
your paths clear-eyed,

finding the far ways up
remembering
to watch

for petals opening
flower heads lifting
after the rain.

Impossibilities

Impossibilities have a wilful kind of life,
sturdier than the certainty of what is.
Wanting to be there to comfort
when the pain is sharpest, knowing
that we will never grow accustomed,
everyday; against that these lucid moments.
Love that sees happiness
in a blue cloud of forget-me-nots,
hope in a small child's "See it! See it!"
as he grapples with the world, the need to tell.
Why dispel all this by listening
to what can never be?
But even the late spring landscape
is mocking in its gentle green, scooping
insistently to valleys edgy with desire.

Desire

is careless,
too imprecise and urgent
for real connections.

What can I call then
this fine flame
stirred by my fingers
on your skin?

A pure blue
startling with heat
it prints you in my head,

kindling an ache exact
enough to trace
each hollow
for the flicker of your pulse.

Travelling

"these two selves who walked half a lifetime untouching"
Adrienne Rich

Sometimes I know we cannot touch
across the hours and years that brought us here.
This moment now so small beside the rest.
We travel separately.
The world inside my head is sometimes safe,
the ghosts familiar, the dangers known,
but I cannot take you there.
I can wake to feel your breath against my face,
drenched in a sleepy warmth that blurs our boundaries,
so close that sometimes now I do not know
if it is happiness I feel, or fear.
So much has gone
into the hours and years that brought us here.
I cannot know where you are travelling,
but I can hold you now, this moment,
while you go.

Parting

*"Parting is such sweet sorrow,
That I shall say goodnight till it be morrow."*

Parting is the world honed down to parting,
nothing sweet, no sorrow but a blind bleak "no"
re-echoing, as Shakespeare knew —
his lovers young, protected from
the bruise and carelessness of everyday.
He tricked them anyway, mixed sleep
with death and seeming-sleep,
soured their sweet sorrow until
they screamed the "no" that recognised mortality.

Beyond a Juliet's clear-eyed hopefulness,
how dare I risk these glints of hope, of clarity,
this unexpected love made rarer
by the sudden snatch of death —
how can I ever part from you without that "no"?

Norfolk Fragments
August 1990

i   Carving quiet morning hours from sleep
I watch the new day creep across dead names.

Rabbits feed untroubled on old mounds, assert
existence in a bolt-eyed concentrated quiver.

A whirring warning heralds partridge, scuttling
flame-red legs in disrespectful outburst.

Under paws and claws rest the Marias and the Alberts.
But what of Anguish, is he peaceful now
in the certain sunlight under warm grey stone?

ii   The landscape offers no escape.
I could be cast on the moon's plain
abandoned starkly.
No curve of hills.
The open sky stares unblinking.
Even the sea has been stretched
into shallow tides,
its crests and tumult beached.

iii   Under a breathless sky
children wearing only skin
crouch digging inlets in hot sand.
Industrious dam builders they miss
the shadows on the ground
absorbed against the after-roar.

The planes cut up the estuary,
sear through August holidays,
practising low flying, targeting.
They'll find it's desert sand on the other side,
and small figures wearing only skin
who crouch absorbed.

iv   The sun has no easy setting,
tugged out of shape,
soft red balloon spilling
across a flat sea.

Darkness is final,
filled with the silent flight of birds,
warmth leaving the earth,
earth turning wind-scraped plain.

But tonight the darkness changed —
watchful — a breath drawn in—
I turned and the moon had risen
to the sun's slow sinking,
globed low and steady,
heavy with quiet light.

Berwick Clifftop, May

Rocks push and break the surface here like bones,
ridges of vertebrae in parallel,
an ancient skeleton enduring while
the cliff tops folded, crumpled far below,
new layers, brave green and the frail gleam of primrose.

Nothing is still, wind stirs the sea to hiss
against the rocks, blue broken into foam —
a blue to speed the heartbeat, catch the breath.
Sun lights an eider duck to shimmering silver,
clear water shows his paddling webs, his arrowhead
sharp cut against the silk-brown weed.

How to accommodate this stretching sea,
these rocks, and summer reawakening
old joys? Hope skims and twists,
strong as the miracle — bright birds returning.

Blue Birds

A flash of colour broke
grey thoughts — two birds
that caught
the evening light.

The underwings gold-brown
but above —
blue like the shimmering inlay
of butterfly wing,
blue like kingfisher,
iridescence dazzling.

But they are nowhere
in the books,
those broad winged
soaring birds — no blue
of that metallic sheen,
no blue birds anywhere.

Alight in angled sunshine
they pulled at me —
what was it
that they promised?

Altitude

It could be climbing
that makes the blood like this —
a reckless racing, brighter red
pushing at the chambers of the heart
until they ache.
It clears the vision to —
each grass blade straining upright
where a boot pressed,
a clarity so sharp
you must stop for a moment
turn round, look back.
The lake is still
white winter light brimming.
It would be beautiful anyway;
a bonus this uncomfortable heart
it won't let you forget.

Dream

The road kept climbing on beyond the place
where I had wondered who would live there.
Warmth left behind with houses, no trace
of farmers' minds upon these crags, rocks bare
and grey as sheep, grey wind to whip a mist
of empty air. High in cold clouds I dream
my home a stone pile in a gully, lost
from the view of passing cars. A woman I dream
moving across a land that does not welcome her.
Her legs grow strong with stumbling, she sees how rocks
are pitted gold with lichen, and her mind grows clear,
her words soar winged, wind-riding, accurate.
She has learned fierce sureness among rocks and air,
I climb back down to you, stronger for being there.

No Flowers

I cannot promise flowers.
Wild flowers belong to summer,
purple loosestrife, meadowsweet, vetch,
ragged robin, clover and pale flax,
old names that conjure clarity,
pure colours, fine lobes and stars,
sharp petals delicately veined,
fragrant and ephemeral.

Summer is past.
This is a time of husks and hidden seeds,
tough shiny evergreens,
the bitter-sweet of nightshade,
white mistletoe's persistent hold.
The fragile flowers are dead
but here are berries rich enough
to see us through.

Ridge

i   I could believe some hand had shaped it,
smoothed and folded, pinched and ridged,
moulding the vertebrae of these hills.
Valleys scooped out, clefts split,
fissures cracked, rocks scattered
to lie lichened and solid,
old grey beasts sleeping.

Then someone tried to contain it.
Patient hands selected stones.
Walls are careful work.
Only the persistent drift
that patterns cloud and light
across solid earth
denies enclosure.

ii   Climbing through late summer
the bracken is tarnished like old gold,
the gorse sharp yellow —
but I am heavy, taste fear
as stones slip, my body not at one
with the hill's rhythm.
The top brings the smell of winter
in an icy wind, austerity
in the far hills' muted tones;
a ridge between seasons, up here
light and transient I breathe joy
in the constancy of rock and sky.

iii   It is not my landscape.
Some spirit stirs impetuous
in the thin cold air
pulling ever higher, drops
in the sudden slips of scree,
from ridge to gully
to the unwrinkled silence of the tarn,
a constant edging towards danger.

A softer spirit
is down there by the stream,
where the path is sheltered,
the sound a gentle washing
over stones, absorbing
an old tranquillity
yet attuned to the ache
of the curlew's cry.

iv   There is no unselfconscious stepping westward,
each path well-trodden by a poet's boot.

Too many poets have seen too much here,
a landscape caught and held responsible,

yet I too would add my layer of mythology,
another contour, a different version.

Harder today to justify this yearning for hills,
the cold wind on the summit cleansing,

that opening up of something in the chest
in the wideness of skies, permanence of rock.

Like chasing a dream, closing the eyes
to grey pavements and brick walls and cars,

I sneak away, carrying consciousness with me,
sharp and uncomfortable on my back.

v   No head for heights
I am drawn here,
a sceptic — one doubt,
one slide of faith
and the path is shale, shifting.

Blood thins, air sings.
Above the silent tarn
birds ride the wind currents
like an image I could use
for this dizzy lift of spirit:

as if it were the first time,
as if it were my vision,
eternity's measure
in the still grey water,
in the ridging backbone
of these hills.

An Autumn Journal

i **In Transit**

Orange light turning
lighting up men who drag
out of the fog at the roadside
some heavy dark thing.
Car walls' metal is too thin.

Fog settles on the heart.
What scent stirred that animal,
blood quickening, insisting
he hazard his purpose
across our lost path?

ii **Colours**

Moving towards the dark time of the year
there are mornings when light does not break.

Mist curls from the cold earth,
clotting the air, breath is fog-heavy.

Bulbs rustle their loose skins,
shelter red petals, sunny yellow heads,

promises of a better time, I bury
them carefully in the dank soil.

Only the trees keep faith, remember
heat and summer in their colours.

Kindling hope and energy their orange
burns against the dead grey sky.

iii *Rhythm*

An ancient rhythm undisturbed,
a message memorised in crust of bark,
knot of root, passed on in fruit and seed,
trees in transition, each colour paced —
an edging towards yellow, aura of orange,
red a hint, and the insistence of slow green.
Their midway point a flaming before death,
they burn out of misty skies and soft decay.

My season. Pulled to these certainties —
the clear-cut shape of tree and leaf —
I print their fire deep inside as if
it could heat, could cauterise and stir
forgotten memories of purposes,
spark the fitful rhythm I have lost.

iv *October Healing*
for Sue

The constancy of old paths,
each fissured rock's endurance,
the gentleness of mist,
cool fingers unravelling the tangle —
this is the only healing.

Your spirit is stirring in its own Spring,
waking from uneasy sleep
to hawthorn bushes alive with birdsong.
In the tongues of Autumn's orange
your voice reclaims its fire.

Conversation

*"The most valuable conversation ... is that which
passes between two friends with their feet on
the fender on winter nights."*
Harriet Martineau

All day they walked
in the rusty crackle of late Autumn,
saw clefts smudged with purple,
winter cut-out trees under thin gold,
the sudden light on water
brimming too clear for words,
conversation broken by the pull of heights
already touched with snow.

Tired now in firelight
they track the stillness singly,
minds washed with colour and wide skies.
There is a moment when silence glows.
Heat hangs in live red caves,
the papery walls breathe in and out
flickering a spark that could turn flame,
could die into the dusty grey of cinders.

Her words are soft moths in darkness
gently blundering
moving towards light.

Crossing the Edge

Mid-December and the season comes clean.
Last night the cut-out clarity of stars
declared it, today the world snapped brittle white.
There is an urgency about the birds,
a flurry of shallow flight, a foraging.
Autumn confused us, mushing the passage;
my breath's cold haze tells me where I am.
We have crossed the edge — no more excuse
for the bulbs or me to send brave shoots
unseasonal, into freezing air.

Letting Love Back

Letting love back in returns
the world to focus.

The foggy monotone of loss
floods with colour.

There are stars again
winter certainty of clear edges.

In focus the stars' cold beauty
in focus guilt   injustice   fear.

The precision of tenderness
knows dumb anguish;

love's safety has no walls against
hunger   hatred   pain;

gentle healing fingers thin
skin to bruising.

Letting love back in returns
the world to focus —

letting the world back in
on love's sharp edge.

Prayer at the Year's Ending

Pale winter sun struggles
in the seep of darkness.
There is not enough light to live by.

Ghosts whisper in shadows,
close in with the dusk.
The past gathers on the year's cusp.

I cannot hold bright moments
in stiff winter fingers.
May hope be safe somewhere, and love.

A season for sleeping, retreating.
I am too cold to touch.
Let the candle's flicker be enough.

CYNTHIA FULLER was born on the Isle of Sheppey in north-east Kent in 1948. Both her maternal grandparents were from Cumberland and her childhood holidays in Allonby on the Solway Firth created a strong bond with the region. After studying at Sheffield University, she lived in Bedford and Aberdeen before moving to Durham in 1980 with David, William and George Fuller. She now feels completely at home in the North East.

She works freelance in education, teaching literature and women's studies for the Open University, and running creative writing workshops for adults. She also works as a writer in schools and colleges. Recently she has been involved in coordinating and writing a course, *Reading Women Writers*, for the National Extension College in conjunction with Virago Press. She is an editor of *Writing Women,* which is produced in Newcastle upon Tyne.

She began to write poetry at school, abandoned it when doing an English degree, and gradually took it up again in the late 1970s. Her poems have appeared in magazines and anthologies, but *Moving Towards Light* is her first collection.